THE OPEN BIBLE FAITH MINISTRIES INC.

Why is Faith Necessary?

Faith Principles for Manifesting Your Prophetic Word

BISHOP DR. TERRENCE PARRIS

PROPHETESS DR. WILLIE MAE PARRIS

COPYRIGHT

DEDICATION

Posthumously submitted after the passing of our daughter, Mary Anitha Parris, on Tuesday, September 2, 2025. Mary submitted these written words for her dad's 30th Ministerial Anniversary while she was touring and performing in the Wizard of Oz.

Congratulations, Daddy, for 30-plus years in ministry! I'm sorry that I'm not there in person to congratulate you and tell you what you mean to me. You are a courageous and dedicated husband, father, and man of God!

I've watched you go above and beyond to help others in their times of need - at times neglecting your own! This is the true attribute of a friend. I watched how you remained strong during trying times, while most would give up, and remained positive. This is an attribute of a leader. I noticed how you were never selfish and shared knowledge and insight with others, when many would hoard the vital concepts to themselves. Only a true mentor will share with others so that they, too, can be enlightened.

Not only do you exhibit the qualities and characteristics of a great leader, mentor, man of God, but you are an amazing father. I just want to thank you for all you have done for me over the past 21 years, and I wish you many more years of ministry, happiness, health, and prosperity. Please stand and show by paying homage to my father, Dr. Terrence Parris.

Happy Anniversary, and I love you!

Mary Anitha Parris

ACKNOWLEDGMENT

Drs. Terrence and Willie Mae Parris would like to thank their many mentors, both spiritually and secularly, and physically, who have impacted, inspired, and enlightened their lives by sharing their knowledge and understanding about the concept of Faith. That Faith was not only a simple word, but a word that demands a corresponding action. Faith is given by God, and everyone has their own measure of Faith that they are responsible for as an individual. It is up to you to grow your Faith. We are so very thankful for learning this life lesson; especially over these past years with our daughter, Mary Anitha Parris. Our Faith continued to remain steadfast and unremovable and anchored in God, His Son, Jesus, and the Holy Spirit.

TABLE OF CONTENTS

ABOUT THE AUTHORS

April 29, 1979 – to Present

Dr. Terrence Parris is the seventh of nine children born to the late Mr. James Edward and Mrs. Anitha Viola Parris. Born in Trinidad, West Indies, he was the youngest student in the graduating class of the Caribbean Bible Institute in 1973. Dr. Terrence Parris is the founder and owner of El-Shaddai Counseling, Consulting, and Training Center. Dr. Parris is a certified mentoring supervisor and has acquired more than 30 years of social work experience in supervision and training. He has conducted workshops and seminars throughout the United States, the West Indies, West Africa, and South America. Dr. Parris is an Ordained Minister, Social Work Consultant, Trainer, and Mentor. He is a graduate of the American International University, the International Theological Seminary of California, New York Theological Seminary, New York University School of Social Work, and the College of New Rochelle. Dr. Parris' ministerial experience is more than 46 years, during which he has served as a Pastor, Teacher, and Prophet. He is also a Board-Certified Pastoral Counselor. Dr. Parris was a faculty member of Touro College for 18 years and the Program Director of Courage to Change, Inc., and a certified Reiki Master, certified Meditation Instructor, NLP Practitioner, certified Life Coach, and certified Chaplain.

Dr. Willie Mae Parris' education and training extend both biblically and secularly. Dr. Parris is a recipient of various certifications, diplomas, and degrees ranging from an Associate of Arts, Bachelor of Arts, Master of Theology/Divinity, Doctor of Theology/Christian Psychology, and a Doctor of Philosophy/Pastoral Psychology. As a licensed minister and evangelical teacher in 1996, the prophetic gift began to stir more readily, and she sought the Master Prophet, Bishop E. Bernard Jordan, and met the Prophetess Debra Jordan on June 4, 1998. The rest is history and no longer a mystery. Dr. Parris, better known as Prophetess Parris, received her ordination as a minister with Zoe Ministries on her 46th Birthday, Sunday, February 22, 2004. Dr. Parris and Prophetess Parris are the founders of the Open Bible Faith Ministries and the International Theological Seminary of New York, as well as the Open Bible Faith College American International University. The Parrises have been married for more than 39 years and had a beautiful daughter, Prophetess Mary Anitha Parris, who was an aspiring Musical Theater performer, Educator, Counselor, and Chaplain. It is with heartfelt sorrow that the Parrises' beloved daughter, Mary Anitha Parris, transitioned on Tuesday, September 2, 2025.

PREFACE

Why Faith is written to help believers in the Lord Jesus Christ understand the scripture Hebrews 11:1 and to eradicate and expand their heart and soul into knowing the difference between believing, hoping, trusting, and exercising the Faith of their very own convictions.

INTRODUCTION
WHY IS FAITH NECESSARY?
FAITH PRINCIPLES FOR MANIFESTING YOUR PROPHETIC WORD

In this study on Faith, we are going to be examining the principles of Faith. What is Faith?

How to walk by Faith? What it means to apply Faith and its results. Through natural Faith, we understand that the hands of God created the world and everything alive. If Jesus said for you to have Faith in God, that means you can have Faith in God. It means that you do not have to struggle to have Faith in God. That means you can have the God kind of Faith to believe God for anything you desire to have according to God's will and purpose for your life.

We learned that what is made possible was made possible because of the profound acts of God. **In Genesis 1:3, And God said, Let there be light: and there was light.** We see God speaking the Word of Faith and creating the galaxies and every other thing under and above the heavens. Do you know that without Faith it is impossible to please God? There are two passages of scripture texts that I would like us to look at for a moment.

Hebrews 11:6 says, But without faith it is impossible to please him: for he that cometh to God must believe that he is, and that he is a rewarder of them that diligently seek him.

Romans 10:17 says, So then faith cometh by hearing, and hearing by the word of God.

These two passages of scripture denote the facts that God is the supreme author of everything and that he spoke to nothing, and something did appear.

NOTES:

CHAPTER 1
FAITH COMETH BY HEARING

> **Principle #1**
>
> **Faith Comes by Hearing the Word of God.**

Faith comes by hearing and hearing by the Word of God. Anything that is impossible is not possible. But without Faith it is impossible to please God. It is impossible to please whom? God! For he that comes to God must first believe, that he is a rewarder of them that diligently seek him. Faith cometh and cometh is not the cometh that the Astrologers talk about. It is not the cometh we observe in the sky every so often. It sounds like the cometh, but Faith cometh, Faith comes, by hearing and hearing by the Word of God. So, Faith comes how? By hearing, and hearing what? "The word of God." I want you to get that principle in your spirit as the foundation is being established. Now, that is the only way Faith comes. And it will be either positive Faith or negative Faith. It must be mountain-moving Faith that will move mountains or Faith that will bring defeat. Faith is not in the past tense; Faith is always in the present tense. Do you know why Faith is always present tense?

Well, the Bible tells us in Hebrews 11:1 now Faith is. What does it say? It says now Faith is. Now is always present. So, if now is always present then Faith is always present. Do you understand that? Faith is not tomorrow, but now. Now! Not tomorrow now, but now, now. Now is not tomorrow, but now. Now is present.

NOTES:

Principle #2

Heard is Past Tense, Hearing is Present Tense.

Heard is the past tense. Yesterday I heard. Heard is the past tense. Now, I am hearing, present tense. Faith is present tense. That is why the Bible says that **faith comes by hearing.**

Hearing is always when? Now, Hearing is always present. You don't say "I was hearing that the other day". It is not correct to say that. That is not present. Even if you were hearing about it the other day, you are still not hearing it now. Do you understand that? So, Faith operates in the arena called now. God is a now God. Our scripture text says, **But without faith, it is impossible to please him.** So, every day in our lives, we must please God, and we please God by Faith. I repeat, we please God every day by Faith. Again, how does Faith come? It comes by hearing and hearing the Word of God. For us to please God, it is very important that we hear the Word of God. That is the only way Faith can come. If we don't hear the Word of God, Faith will not come.

NOTES:

Principle #3

There are a Positive Side and a Negative Side to Faith.

There are a positive side and a negative side to Faith. And everything you hear will either build Faith in you, that is positive, or bring glory to God, and will allow you to trust God, or negative Faith that will trust in the things of this world.

A good example of what I am talking about is television. The television industry is famous for building Faith in our lives. Remember what you hear will affect you.

Subliminal messages are designed to have serious impact on us. Now, whenever you sit down to watch TV, as you are accustomed. You will be entertained by several advertisements which are designed to send subliminal messages to you. For example, I love peas and rice. I may be sitting down eating a delicious plate of peas and rice, and the TV may be playing an advertisement, describing pasta and meatballs.

Now, I am not a lover of pasta and meatballs. But, while I was eating something I love and heard that subliminal message, the next time I am in the grocery store, minding my own business, pasta and meatballs will invade the privacy of my mind and have me walk over to the pasta and meatball and pick it up.

Now, where are the pasta and meatballs? In my shopping cart.

It was only because I heard the advertisement about pasta and meatballs that registered in my consciousness before I got to the grocery store that made me purchase the pasta and meatballs. You see, when we hear things, they register in our spirit, and our spirit receives it and accepts it. Faith is activated by what we see. Once I saw the pasta and meatballs, my desire for them was activated. Do you see that? So that is why it is so important for you to hear the Word of God. If you don't hear the Word of God, you are going to develop a Faith that is negative, and it will destroy you. That is why so many of God's People lose their testimony.

NOTES:

Why do you think so many Christians get involved in occult practices? Well, it is simple because of what they heard. Every time you hear the Word of God, Faith comes. Whenever you hear the Word of God, you can act on the Word, and Faith comes.

Whatever you hear, you can accept it, believe it, and act on it. Do you see that? Biblical Faith comes by hearing the Word of God. Every time you hear the Word of God, Faith will come. I know a lot of people in the Church are guilty of this crime called doubt. I was guilty of this at one time. I used to be so guilty of it; I mean, God brings revelation to me now. Thank God for freedom from guilt. Oh, "I heard that before". The Bible never said that Faith comes by hearing it before. Think about that. You might be guilty of this yourself. You probably said it a few minutes ago, an hour ago, and yesterday or the day before. The point of the matter is, we all at some point in our walk with the Lord have said, "Oh! I heard that before". So, if I heard that before, I don't have to hear it again.

Well! Faith doesn't work like that. God never said that Faith comes by having heard the Word or by reading the Word in the sense of reading the Word. For I believe a measure of Faith comes when we read the Word of God.

NOTES:

During my early years of ministry, I left a worship service prematurely because when the minister mentioned his subject, I said to myself, "I have heard this message so many times". Why am I here? This minister's topic will always be entitled "GOD IS". All my negative thoughts about this pastor's messages had not benefited me because of my ignorance of Faith at that time. Now, that was foolishness on my part.   That was acting out of ignorance on my part. Not knowing is a dangerous thing. And not knowing when we think we know is more dangerous. I thought I knew what he was going to say. I underestimated God in man. I realized how immature I was in the Word. God can speak a Word even when we have failed to do as he commanded because Faith comes by hearing and hearing by the Word of God.

NOTES:

Principle #4

Faith Works by Acting on The Word of God.

Faith works by acting on the Word of God. We can only act on the Word that we hear. The Word we hear will be either positive or negative. So, let us examine how your Faith works. You are on your way home from a great, wonder-working service. The anointing of God was present, and the whole House of God was blessed. So, you are on your way home from this service. You are minding your own business, singing and making a joyful noise unto the Lord. Suddenly, you are challenged with the noise of a blasting music truck playing Killing Me Softly with its song, telling my whole world that he loves me, with his song... Now, remember you are minding your own business, praying and singing in the spirit. As you continue along your way, for some reason, you're not praying and singing in the spirit anymore. You are now caught up on another plane singing another song. This time, you're not singing Jehovah Nissi, or Jehovah Jireh, but you are singing Killing Me Softly. Distraction from the outer world is designed to take you away from your focus on God. During the time that you were not praying and singing in the spirit, you were being entertained by other thoughts that got into your ears and into your spirit.

NOTES:

Faith Works by Acting on The Word of God.

Now, remember your ear is a doorway to the spirit. You are now home and taking your shower, feeling good about yourself. You start singing again, this time you are not singing worship music like Jehovah Jireh or Jehovah Nissi, but you have now gone back in time with Killing Me Softly with its song. So, what happened? The song got into your spirit. What happened? Faith comes by hearing whatever you hear. Be it positive or negative. What type of Faith came? "Negative Faith" that will not be pleasing to God.

Satan doesn't want you to please God. He wants to be pleased. He has his own little god kingdom that he is trying to build. His little gods are the ones that are distracting you.

By the spirit of the moment, Faith comes, but not godly Faith or positive Faith, not the Faith that pleases God, but the Faith that pleases Satan. You see, my brothers and sisters, this is the way the enemy operates in this world, through our thoughts and actions. No one is exempt from this scheme of the evil one. But the good thing above this is that you don't have to fall prey to his schemes. The Bible says to resist the devil, and he shall flee from you.

There is a positive and a negative side to Faith. Faith that pleases God comes from His Word because God and His Word are one. How do you know that God and His Word are one? Because the bible says it in *John 1:1says, In the beginning was the Word, and the Word was with God, and the Word was God.*

Do you see how everything is directly linked to the Word? Think about this for a moment. Do you understand why you cannot live without the Word in your life? Think about the Christians you know who are without the Word, a regular part of their life. Remember to pay close attention to the words that you speak because death and life are in the power of your tongue. You must be sure of yourself when it comes to what you say and how you say it. Someone is always listening to your words.

NOTES:

Principle #5

Faith Does Not Come by Just Reading the Word of God.

Faith does not come by just reading the Word of God. That is the deception the enemy uses to have Christians believe. He probably has you believing the same thing.

Well, if Faith doesn't come by reading, how does it come? It comes by hearing the Word of God. To hear is different from reading, although when you read, you hear yourself in the quietness of your mind. But that is not what I am referring to when I say, "Faith comes by hearing." I am not talking about hearing when you are reading. What happens when you read?

When you read, you receive revelation. Revelation of what the revealed Word of God is saying to you and your situation. The Word revealed to us is the revelation you would experience as you read the Word of God. So, revelation comes by reading. Faith comes by hearing the Word of God. It is important for you to hear and read the Word of God on a regular basis. How do you receive revelation through the reading of the Word? The Holy Spirit will reveal the Word to you. This happens because you are a spirit. And that which is spirit and born of the spirit can understand the things of the spirit. God's Word is spirit and life. For you to receive revelation of God's Word, you must be born of his spirit and make reading His Word a daily habit.

NOTES:

CHAPTER 2
THE OBJECT OF FAITH IS GOD

Principle #6
The Object of Faith is God.

The object of Faith is God. Without God, you cannot have Faith. And without Faith you cannot please God. Remember that God and His Word is one. They are inseparable.

Mark 11:22-24 says, And Jesus answering said unto them, Have Faith in God. Which God? The God of this world, No! God Almighty! Now I want you to keep this in mind. There are two rulers of this world. There is the God of this world, Satan, and the God of all creation, Jehovah God. Some people have Faith in the God of this world. Someone earlier today told me that tonight there is a big concert in New York with a theme called "The Grateful Dead". Who do you think the participants at this concert will be giving worship too? What God would they be giving glory too? Satan. Where is the object of your Faith?

The bible says in *Mark 11:23 For verily I say unto you, that whosoever shall say unto this mountain, be thou removed, and be thou cast into the sea; and shall not doubt in his heart, but shall believe that those things which he saith shall come to pass; he shall have whatsoever he saith.*

What did the Word say for you to do? It said for you to speak to the mountain. It never said for you to climb the rough side of the mountain, as the favorite song says to do.

Deception! Deception! Deception! What are we to do to the mountain? We are to speak to the mountain, say to the mountain, "Be thou removed in Jesus' name".

I am not climbing any rough side of any mountain when my God tells me different.

God told me to speak to the mountain, and the mountain shall go. Hallelujah. Whatever position the mountains are in your lives, you must speak to those mountains, and they shall be removed. The mountains originated from a place. Therefore, you must speak to that mountain and send it back to the place it came from. You tell it to go in Jesus' name. You talk to it like that. You tell it to get out.

NOTES:

Principle #7

Mountains are Anything in Your Life That Hinder You.

Mountains are anything in your life that hinders you. For example, mountains can be sickness. The Word of God tells you that by his stripes you were healed. So, if you are healed by his stripes and you believe God's Word, then if you confess sickness, you are telling God that he is a liar. Do you see that? Do you understand that? Just think about this for a moment. The Word of God is truth. And God's Word says that by his stripes we are healed. So, when you are attacked in your body through sickness and diseases, if you cling to those sicknesses and diseases and accept them, you are saying to God that His Word is not true, and there is no validity to His Word.

You are saying that God is a liar. And he lied. God is not glorified when you are sick, as some believe. God is not glorified when your family is sick. He is not glorified in that situation. You might give God praise while you are battling with your sickness, but do you really think that God is glorified in your situation? No, I don't believe that He is glorified in your sickness when He sent His Word and healed all your diseases. What glory can sickness bring to God?

God never said that you would never be attacked. However, he said in His Word for you to rebuke the devourer. You don't have to accept Satan's thoughts of sickness and disease. I will give you an example of how to rebuke sickness.

NOTES:

Principle #7
Mountains are Anything in Your Life That Hinder You.

One Sunday, just before I had to minister the Word, my wife and my daughter were attacked by the enemy. They somehow started having symptoms of the flu. Well, I said to myself, devil, you are a liar from the pit of hell, and today you are not going to have any victory over me or my family. I continued to say in the name of Jesus Christ, I am the head of this house, and you have no place in here; therefore, I command you by the power invested in me and by the blood of Jesus, get out of my family and my household. You are not going to prevent me from ministering the Word of God.

I went and ministered the Word, and when I returned home, my wife and my daughter were up and running around, feeling better and rejoicing. My daughter was running a fever of 104 degrees, and just like that, swiftly and quickly, her fever left. Hallelujah.

I anointed her with the oil of joy and healing, and I release my Faith on my child's behalf. This is my seed; therefore, I command fever to go. What did you think happened? The fever left immediately. We took her to the doctor the next day. The doctor took her temperature, and it was normal. Now, that is Faith in action, not climbing up the rough side of the mountain. Why waste God's precious time, when He said to say it, believe it, and do it. Speak to that mountain in Jesus' name.

NOTES:

Principle #8

Disbelief is One of The Greatest Mountains A Christian Must Struggle With.

Disbelief is one of the greatest mountains you must struggle with as a child of the Lord. Did you know that disbelief is a mountain? Well, let me inform you that disbelief is telling God that He is a liar and His Word is not the truth. Disbelief will cause burdens in your life. It will cause you to develop strongholds in every area of your Christian Walk and witness for the Lord. Disbelief can become an imagination, which can become a stronghold in your life. The Bible says to cast down imaginations. God wants you to do that. It brings Him glory when you can cast down the imagination of unbelief. God is a God of indifference. He is no respecter of persons. What he will do for others, he will do for you. Do you know that if God were a respecter of persons, what that would mean? It will mean that God would have favorites. And that is not the case with God. He does not have favorites. What he does have are his children, who are experiencing more of his divine favor because of their relationship with him and their knowledge of his plan for their lives. Thank God for his goodness. Whatever he would do for you, he would do for me. Now, only God's children who are born of the Spirit of God can please him. Not everyone in this world is a child of God. We are all his creation, but we are not all his children. We are his creation, because God is the creator, but we are not all children of the Most-High. We are not all sons of God. There is the God of this world, and he has his children, too, the children of disobedience. God gave you and me the privilege to become sons of God. He qualified us. Thank God! So, you see, only those who are in Christ and are children can please Him.

NOTES:

Not everyone is a qualified child of God. Just because everybody is going around saying, "I am a child of the King, I am a Christian," doesn't make a person a Christian.

In Christianity, too many people are just going to Church. I mentioned recently that if you go to the mall and if you ask the question, are you a Christian to several people, you will get several different types of answers. And you know it could be simply one of these three.

You would get those who say "yes, I believe in God", " yes, I go to church", or "yes, I read my bible". But they rarely answer "yes, I am a Christian". Some of you reading this book now believe that going to church automatically makes you, as well as qualifies you to be a Christian. Reading the Bible or praying to God doesn't make you a Christian. The Bible gives you and me one way to become a child of God. And that is by salvation. *Acts 4:12 says, Neither is there salvation in any other: for there is none other name under heaven given among men, whereby we must be saved.*

So, the object of your Faith is God the Father, God the Son, and God the Holy Spirit.

NOTES:

John 1:12 says, But as many as received him, to them gave he power to become the sons of God, even to them that believe on his name: Do you see that? This is referring to the Son. So, you see, you cannot get away from the Son, the middleman in the blessed Trinity, the Christ, your mediator, Lord, and king. Now, let us look at what *Romans 8:12-14 says, Therefore, brethren, we are debtors, not to the flesh, to live after the flesh.*

13. For if ye live after the flesh, ye shall die: but if ye through the Spirit do mortify the deeds of the body, ye shall live. 14. For as many as are led by the Spirit of God, they are the sons of God. It says for as many as believed if I were to tell you as many people, I would be talking about a great number that cannot be counted. It says for as many that are led by whose Spirit. "The spirit of God". They are the Sons of God. For as many as are led by the Spirit of God. The Spirit of God is referring to the Holy Spirit. Do you understand that? Again, here we see the Blessed Trinity as modeled as the object of Faith.

NOTES:

Principle #10

The Nature of Faith is The Acceptance of God's Word as Truth.

The nature of God's Word is the acceptance of the Word of God as truth. That is the nature of Faith. Yes! I mean accepting the Word of God as God speaking *to* you, His truth. I want to show you by way of the Word of God that you cannot live any other way but by Faith. If you don't believe me, just read what the logos (the living Word says).

Habakkuk 2:4 says, Behold, his soul which is lifted up is not upright in him: but the just shall live by his faith. Who are the just? The just are the righteous. The righteous are the just ones who are born again of the Spirit of the Living God. They are reborn by Faith in Jesus Christ. The child of God's Walk is a walk of Faith. Doing everything by Faith in the unadulterated Word of God. You and I are now to do everything by Faith and trust, and not through presumption. Now Faith is very important to the believer. But a lot of believers speak negatively when it comes to speaking about Faith. Well, Faith is not a movement. There is no such thing as a Faith movement. I personally don't believe in any Faith movement. I do believe what the Bible says concerning Faith and the believer's life. That is "you" the believer cannot live without Faith.

NOTES:

Principle #10

The Nature of Faith is The Acceptance of God's Word as Truth.

You cannot come to God without acknowledging your Faith in Him. Faith is everything. Every message is a Faith message. Every action is a Faith action. Faith is pleasing to God. You cannot get away from Faith.

Romans 1:17 says, For therein is the righteousness of God revealed, from faith to faith:

As it is written, **the just shall live by faith.**

Are you a just one? Are you living by Faith? Did you receive the measure of Faith? Well, you are the righteousness of God, created in Christ Jesus for the glory of God. You should live by Faith so that you can demonstrate God on this planet earth, so that you can demonstrate your I Am nature, the nature of God in you. Remember, you and God are one. There is no separation from God's side of the evidence if you are a son of God.

The fact of the matter is God said it in His Word, and he cannot lie. He is all truth. So, trust in His Word. Because God and His Word are one, and you and the Word are one.

CHAPTER 3
THE JUST SHALL LIVE BY FAITH

> **Principle #11**
>
> **Don't Draw Back on Your Faith. God Always has Your Back.**

Don't draw back. You have come too far to turn around. God always has your back. *Hebrews 10:38 says, Now the just shall live by Faith, but if any man draw back, my soul shall have no pleasure in him.* When shall the just live by Faith? Now! Not in eternity, but now. You would not need Faith there. You will have everything that you need already. So, you would not have a need for it. You will be the bridegroom to the bride. There will be one great big feast where the bride and you will be one with everyone. Thank God. We would not have to do any preparation then because the preparation would have already been done while living on the earth. Who has done the preparation? The bride has made this preparation. Tradition says that the bride takes on the responsibility of the wedding plans for her wedding. That is tradition but thank God we have everything already planned. Do you know that God loves pleasure? God is a personality. That is why He can enjoy the pleasure you give to him. You bring God glory and praise that is pleasurable to Him. So, don't give up now. You must continue to fight a good fight of Faith as the Apostle Paul did, looking to Jesus the Christ, the Holy One, the Mighty One, the Prince of Peace, the Everlasting Father, and the Great I Am.

NOTES:

Principle #12

Action Speaks Louder Than Words.

Faith is action. It is acting on what God said in His Word. The Bible says that your Faith will demonstrate your actions. Many times, we will tell ourselves that we have Faith, but we don't do anything that demonstrates that we have the Faith we are declaring. In other words, we don't act on what we say. The Bible says that Faith without work is dead.

Faith needs action for it to be manifested. Your Faith must be put into action, or it will not manifest anything. You cannot have Faith without corresponding action. Faith and belief are two different things. You can believe something and not have Faith in it. But Faith is always action. It is always taking the next step. Let us examine some examples of Faith in action. *Hebrews 12:2 says, Looking unto Jesus, the author and finisher of our faith, who for the joy that was set before Him, endured the cross, despising the shame, and is set now at the right hand of the throne of God.*

So, who is the author and finisher of your Faith? Jesus Christ.

NOTES:

And if you are the author of something, you are the engineer of it. You are the prime purpose for it. Now the Bible says looking unto Jesus. So how are we to look unto Jesus? You must look unto Jesus with Faith, because Jesus Christ is Faith. The Bible says that he is the finisher of your Faith. Revelations says he is the Alpha and the Omega, meaning that he is the beginning and the end. So, there is no way you and I can get around Jesus. Because Jesus is the beginning and the end, and the best part of all of this is that he is the in-between, too. Jesus is the fullness of God. So, Christ is the source of my Faith, and your Faith. There is no getting around that fact and truth. We cannot get anywhere without Faith. You and I were saved because of Faith. Show me a Christian who is saved without Faith. Faith is what determines the character of a Christian and a non-Christian. A non-Christian can only be saved by Faith, godly Faith, and the God kind of Faith.

NOTES:

Everyone born on this earth is born with Faith. Do you believe that? But when we were dead in sins, our Faith was not active. It was not activated or came alive. Your Faith and my Faith became alive when you and I believed in the power of Jesus Christ. When we accepted him as Lord and Savior, our Faith became alive. Our Faith became alive when God infused his Faith with our Faith (human Faith).

Romans 12: 3 for I say, through the grace given unto me, to every man that is among you, not to think of himself more highly than he ought to think; but to think soberly, according as God hath dealt to every man the measure of Faith. You received a measure of Faith, but you must add to the measure you received. How do you add to the measure you received? Well, you must study to show yourself approved unto God. You must spend time in prayer and supplication. You must have fellowship with God. You must spend time fasting and meditating on the Word. You were born with what I call human Faith or trust within intuition.

For example, when a baby is given a bottle and takes a sip of the contents in that bottle, and then continues to drink without hesitation, that baby drinks the liquid content based on trust and Faith. Now that the baby trusts you and drinks whatever is in the bottle with the measure of Faith they were given. So, they have Faith. The God kind of Faith is implanted in your human spirit when you come into the reality of who Christ is. This took place when you became a child of God through your birth. I know people who are hardcore sinners. They have Faith. But their Faith is not the kind of Faith that you and I have.

NOTES:

They don't have the God kind of Faith which comes through Jesus. They have Faith in otherness or the devil. They have the Faith of the devil. They have the counterfeit; you and I have the real thing. You have the kind of Faith that moves mountains. All you must do is speak to the mountains in your lives and tell them to go in Jesus' name, and the mountains shall go. You see, the world has the kind of Faith that tells them to go and climb the rough side of the mountain. You see, the Bible never tells us to climb any kind of mountains. It never told us to climb a rough or a smooth mountain. Thank you, Jesus!

It says to speak to the mountain, and the mountain will be removed and cast into the sea. How sad it is to know that people think that climbing the rough side of the mountain will glorify God. That is not walking and acting in Faith. That is acting out of foolishness and assumption. That is not God's will for his children. We all start off at the same point, but we don't get to the finish line together. And God has given us the measure of Faith so that we can build upon that measure. Add to your measure virtue; add to your measure knowledge. How do you add to your measure? Well! You see, you can add to your Faith by first knowing that God did not give you a spirit that is separated from Him. He placed within you, His spirit. He did not give you a spirit of fear but of power, love, and a sound mind. Faith comes by hearing and hearing by the Word of God.

NOTES:

Principle #13

Everyone Was Born with a Measure of Faith.

So, every time you and I hear the Word of God, we are adding to our Faith. And when you act on what you hear, you are also adding to your Faith. Do you see and understand that? At one point in time, I used to sit in congregational meetings, and I would say to myself and wonder why this preacher was doing such miracles. This man was doing much for God. I honestly thought that God had given him more than he had given me. But you must understand this about this minister, he was spending time with God and communicating with Him, and I wasn't. We started out together. But while he was running, I was taking my time. He had energy because of the time spent in prayer; I was dragging because of the lack of prayer. He was building his Faith with the Word of God.

He was reading the Word of God. While he was doing all of this, he was hearing the Word of God, and his Faith was built up. You can hear the Word when you read the Word.

When you can start talking Faith to yourself and talking the Word to yourself, you will start quoting the Word to yourself. Do you know what will happen? Faith will then rise in you. This happened to me while traveling on a bus. And what did I do? I started to quote the scriptures. I felt like a giant rose up in me. When I got to my destination, there was an incident occurring that only God knew, but he was preparing me in advance for it. I had to stand on Faith and crush the enemy's head. I was quoting scriptures, and I didn't know where they were coming from. I believe they were coming from within my spirit. I didn't have it in my mind to do that. Faith comes, and you will have acted.

NOTES:

CHAPTER 4

FAITH IS A LETHAL WEAPON

Principle #14

Faith is a Christian's Lethal Weapon.

The Word of God in the believer's mouth is a lethal weapon. When used appropriately can be a great force against the enemy. Let us look at what *2 Kings 5:1 says, Now Naaman, captain of the host of the king of Syria, was a great man with his master, and honorable, because by him the Lord had given deliverance unto Syria: he was also a mighty man of valor, but he was a leper.*

As we see here, Naaman was a leper. So, with all the good things he had and was, he was still an unclean man. He was a man of valor, but he was a leper. He was considered unclean. In biblical times, the lepers were put on an Island by themselves. No one came near them. When a person had leprosy, they had their own street to walk on. They also had to announce that they were lepers so that no one would meet them, and they would not encounter others. You see, that is how it was during those times. That is how prejudiced the people were at that time. The leper had to announce himself. And when the leper was healed, the leper had to go to the priest, and the priest had to pronounce and confirm that the leper was healed and that it was ok for them to go on.

Now, Naaman was a man of valor. This meant that he was a man of great respect and honor. But let us look at what happened. *Verse 2 says, And the Syrians had gone out by the companies, and had brought away captive out of this land of Israel, a little maid; and she waited on Naaman's wife. Verse 3 And she said unto her mistress, Would God my lord were with the prophet that is in Samaria! for he will recover him of his leprosy.*

NOTES:

Principle #14

Faith is a Christian's Lethal Weapon.

This woman heard about the Prophet of Samaria. There were many Prophets in Samaria, and the people believed in the spoken words of the prophets. The Prophets were the men and women of God during that time in biblical history. If you wanted to hear from God, the Prophet would give you the Word. So, you see, this maid was telling Naaman's wife that the man of God would be able to cure him from leprosy. *Verse 4-8 says,*

4. And one went in, and told his lord, saying, Thus and thus said the maid that is of the land of Israel.

5. And the king of Syria said, Go to, go, and I will send a letter unto the king of Israel. And he departed, and took with him ten talents of silver, and six thousand pieces of gold, and ten changes of raiment.

6. And he brought the letter to the king of Israel, saying, Now when this letter is come unto thee, behold I have therewith sent Naaman my servant to thee, that thou mayest recover him of his leprosy.

7. And it came to pass, when the king of Israel had read the letter, that he rent his clothes and said, Am I God, to kill and to make alive, that this man doth send unto me to recover a man of his leprosy? Wherefore consider, I pray you, and see how he seeketh a quarrel against me.

8. And it was so, when Elisha the man of God had heard that the king of Israel had rent his clothes, that he sent to the king, saying, Wherefore hast thou rent thy clothes? let him come now to me, and he shall know that there is a prophet in Israel.

NOTES:

Do you see that? They were putting pressure on the king. The king was concerned about what was happening. The king wasn't a priest, so the king could not authorize or affirm Naaman as clean or whole. He had power, but not the power to declare healing to anyone. The priest was the authority in this area of gifting. Why go to Samaria when there is a prophet in Israel? You see, this is like some of us in the kingdom of God. God will tell you to do something you are not familiar with doing. When you do what God tells you to do, you will see the miracle-working power of God demonstrated in your life. You will begin to witness for yourself the power of God in action. You will begin to experience the anointing of God upon your life like never before, taking you into areas of the unknown in God's abundance and riches he has planned for you. You will also begin to know that you are the entire God there is to know on this planet and in the realm of the spirit. You will begin to manifest the presence of God and walk in the authority of your divine self. Then, will the power of God that manifested back in biblical times reappear again in this dispensation of God's Grace.

NOTES:

9. So Naaman came with his horses and with his chariot, and stood at the door of the house of Elisha.

10. And Elisha sent a messenger unto him, saying, Go and wash in Jordan seven times, and thy flesh shall come again to thee, and thou shall be clean.

11. But Naaman was wroth, and went away, and said, Behold, I thought he will surely come out to me, and stand, and call on the name of the Lord his God, and strike his hand over the place, and recover the leper.

Naaman wanted Elisha to personally come and anoint him, and have all this done unto him, but did God say to have this done? No! he didn't. God's instructions through the Prophet of God were for Naaman to go and dip seven times in the water, in Jordan's river, and your flesh shall come again to thee, and thou shall be made whole. A double-blessing miracle was planned by God for Naaman. Now, you see, Naaman was angry and all twisted. He had an attitude that was not pleasing to God. He didn't want to do as he was told by God through the Prophet of God. He was set on having the Prophet to come and personally minister to him. He wanted to have the Prophet to lay hands upon him and call on the name of the Lord, but the Prophet did what the Lord told him to do. That was to tell him to go and dip seven times in Jordan's River, and he would recover How did he respond? Let us now examine what he did.

NOTES:

12. Are not Abana and Pharpar, rivers of Damascus, better than all the waters of Israel? may I not wash in them, and be clean? So, he turned and went away in a rage.

Apparently, Naaman had an experience with the Jordan River that he didn't want to be dipping there. Maybe the water was not clean and was filthy. Maybe he knew of better, cleaner water, or maybe he just didn't want to go to the Jordan River. He began to rationalize and said to himself, if I must go and dip in the river, maybe I can go and dip in another river where there is cleaner water. Little did he know that God always has the final Word in our life's situation. Sometimes we don't understand how God works in our lives and in nature. I would think that anyone in the natural realm would want to do the same as Naaman. Imagine you have clean water in your town, and you must go to another township and dip in dirty water. That is human nature's natural response.

God will tell us to walk south and we walk north. God will tell us to sit down and we stand up. God will tell us to close our eyes, and we open them. How many times does the Word of prophesy go forth to give us direction for our live and we stay the same way?

It's human nature. Naaman was no different than you and I. He was a man of valor. He was a man of good report. He was an honorable man. He knew God's power to some degree.

NOTES:

13. And his servant came near, and spake unto him, and, My father, if the prophet had bid thee do some great thing, wouldest thou not have done it? how much rather then, when he saith to thee, Wash, and be clean?

Most of us only want to hear the good things the Prophet says. But when the Prophet says that God is going to rebuke you and God is going to whip you and chastise you, you don't want to hear that Word. That is one of the greatest problems in Christendom today. A lot of you will respond to the prophetic Word just as Naaman did. Now! Let's look at this example. If God were to speak a prophetic word to you about fire and brimstone that is heading your way, you would want to ask, "Is this God?" This would be the first thought on your mind. All the time God is giving you prophecy about directions in your life, and all the good that is coming your way that God was going to do, and then you say, wow, what did I do to anger God?

Well! You see that human nature to think like that. But this is not the way God thinks about you. Yes! That is what I am saying! God does not think of you in that manner. Sometimes it is very difficult for you to accept and believe the prophetic Word. On 10/08/93, I gave a prophetic word to a young lady who visited our ministry. When she received the prophetic Word, she did not understand what the Lord was saying to her. So, she called me at my home for prophetic counseling regarding the prophetic Word she had received. You see, this young lady wanted to hear what she created in her mind. But it was not what the Lord wanted her to know. God spoke to her what she needed to hear, and it was in the right season of her life. After our phone conversation and my explaining various aspects of the prophetic Word to her, she finally understood what God was saying to her. Two weeks to the date of our conversation, she called me and indicated that everything that was said in the prophetic Word concerning her life and the situation she was involved with came to pass exactly as the prophetic Word stated. Now, this young lady was a pastor.

NOTES:

Faith is a Christian's Lethal Weapon.

14. Then went he down, and dipped himself seven times in Jordan, according to the saying of the man of God: and his flesh came again like unto the flesh of a little child and he was clean.

So, after Naaman rationalized concerning where he should go and dip, he finally accepted the prophetic Word for his life and decided to follow the directions of God's Word and dipped in the river Jordan seven times. Suppose he had dipped once, twice, three or four, five or even six times, what do you think would have happened? Do you think he would have been healed and clean? Absolutely not! In that moment, he realized that the only way for him to be fully recovered and be made clean was to obey the Prophet and live. So, he did and dipped seven times in the river Jordan and was made clean. Sometimes the Prophet will tell you to do some things that will appear out of this world. They will tell you something that will not be understood for some time. But just believe the Prophet and you shall prosper. You see, God works in mysterious ways, but his mysterious ways you will understand. Thank you, Father God in Jesus, the Christ.

NOTES:

Principle #15

God Will Always do What He Says He Will Do.

Now, if God tells you to go and take a dip in Coney Island, would you go and dip? Or if he said for you to go and take spit and make some clay and place it over your body, would you do it? You see, God works in mysterious ways. Ways that you and I don't understand. Sometimes God talks to me, and I wonder and ponder what he is saying.

I must sometimes ask myself, God, is that you? After a while, and after you start to demonstrate your Faith and begin to act on Faith and God's Word, you will be able to tune yourself to God speaking or God's language. You will know when God is talking to you. God speaks to himself. Therefore, when he speaks to you, he is speaking to himself.

You and I, we are the workmen for God on this earth. God cannot do anything without his man. Whenever God tells you to do a thing for him, he will back you up with His Word. His Word will never return unto him void of what it was sent out to do. God is waiting for you to demonstrate his power through you. He is waiting for you to manifest his name and his power. His name and his power must be manifested through you because you are his crowned masterpiece here on earth, displaying his beauty and power, excellence and grace, his honor and mercy, his abundance and wisdom to display.

NOTES:

Principle #16

Faith Must be Demonstrated by Your Actions.

Faith must have corresponding action for it to have a positive effect. The man at the pool of Siloam is a good example of Faith in action.

John 9: 6-7 says, 6 When he had thus spoken, he spat on the ground, and made clay of spittle, and he anointed the eyes of the blind man with the clay, 7 and said unto him, Go, wash in the pool of Siloam, (which is by interpretation, Sent.) He went his way therefore, and washed, and came seeing.

Who told this blind man to take the following steps and follow the instructions given? It was Jesus, the Christ. What did Jesus say for him to do? He told him to go and wash. What did Jesus do before he told him to go and wash? Jesus spat on the ground and made clay of the spittle, and then he anointed the eyes of the blind man with the clay that was made and told him to go wash in the pool of Siloam. Now, what happened after this blind man followed all the instructions given by Jesus? He, the blind man, came seeing. The blind man's action was to go and wash in the pool of Siloam. He was not to go to Blue Mountain pool, nor Pleasant Grove pool, nor Healing Streams pool, but to the pool of Siloam. The blind man went and did as he was told. And, because of his obedience to the words of the master prophet Jesus, the Christ, he was made clean. His action was manifested when he left where he was and went to the pool of Siloam. There, he understood his encounter with God.

NOTES:

CHAPTER 5

THERE IS POWER TO HEAL WHEN THE PRESENCE OF THE LORD IS PRESENT

> Principle #17
>
> **The Power Must be Present.**

Luke 5: 17-21 says, And it came to pass, on a certain day, as he was teaching, that there were Pharisees and doctors of the Law sitting by, which were come out of every town of Galilee, and Judea, and Jerusalem: and the power of the Lord was present to heal them.

The presence of the lord was present, and where his presence is, there is the power to heal.

You see, when the power of the lord is present, there is unlimited power for divine intervention and blessings.

18. And behold, men brought in a bed a man which was taken with a palsy; and they sought means to bring him in, and to lay him before him.

That mean they could not come in the main entrance, because the main entrance was packed with people waiting to go in to receive of the Lord. Those men who brought the sick man were determined to get inside that building.

19. And when they could not find by what way they might bring him in because of the multitude, they went upon the housetop, and let him down through the tiling with his couch into the midst before Jesus.

These men had to rip the tiles up. Think about this action, just picture what is going on in that environment. Imagine a man coming through the ceiling!

NOTES:

20. And when he saw their faith, he said unto him, Man, thy sins are forgiven thee.

When he saw their Faith, whose Faith? Their Faith, the sick man's Faith, as well as those men who took him to the rooftop. There is plural! When Jesus saw their Faith, what did he say to them? He said, ***man thy sins are forgiven***. Imagine Jesus talking like one of the boys.

Man, thy Faith has healed you. Go thy way and sin no more! I want you to get this revelation in your spirit. It says, "and when he saw their Faith, he said unto him," Jesus could not just use the word man without emphasis. He couldn't just use the Word and say Man, go thy way, your Faith has made you whole. Jesus probably said, ***Man, go thy way, your Faith has healed you!*** He had to say it.

You see what happened here was Jesus was operating in the gift of Faith. This was an aggressive statement. When you say the word man to give a message, you don't say it like you're scared and without authority. You say it with authority, knowing that Jesus and all of heaven got you back.

After Jesus affirmed the healing of the sick man, look what happened.

21. And the scribe and the Pharisees began to reason saying, Who is this which speaketh blasphemies? Who can forgive sins, but God alone?

They thought Jesus was speaking blasphemies because Jesus' voice was so strong, the gift of Faith came upon him as he said to the man go, thy Faith has healed you. Your sins are forgiven. The Pharisees started reasoning amongst themselves, asking, who is this man? Who is he to forgive sin? Only God can forgive sin. The Pharisees were too far to see the goodness of the Lord. Jesus did not mention anything concerning the sick man's Faith. What he did say was their Faith. So, if he was referring to their Faith, he was referring to the men who brought the man down, and those there in the room as a corporate body. Do you see that?

CHAPTER 6
GOD'S POWER IN HIS WORD

> Principle #18
>
> **You Cannot be Saved Without Faith**.

God's power is in His Word. The Faith of God is the power of God. I want you to know that you cannot be saved without Faith. And, not only that, but the Word of God, which is the Word of Faith, is near us. Romans 10:8-9 says,

8. But what saith it? The word is nigh thee, even in thy mouth, and in thy heart: that is the word of faith, which we preach;

9. that if thou shalt confess with thy mouth the Lord Jesus, and shalt believe in thine heart that God hath raise Him from the dead, thou shalt be saved.

The first thing I want to make clear to you is that you cannot be saved without Faith. That is a fact. And I repeat, the Word of Faith is the Word of God, which is near you, in your mouth. The Word of Faith is so close to you that it is in your mouth. And not only in your mouth, but it is in your heart. Look at these two words, the mouth and the heart. The Bible says that which comes out of the mouth is what you have in your heart. When something comes from the heart, what exit does it take? It exits through the mouth. So, pay close attention to those two words, the mouth and the heart, because with the heart, man believeth, and with the mouth, confession is made. Do you see the connection between the mouth and the heart? If there weren't a mouth, then the heart would have nothing to confess. If there is no heart, then there is nothing to believe in. So, the mouth and the heart are partners. One you believe with and the other you say it with. God demonstrated this same principle back in Genesis. Do you know that God spoke the Word? He spoke His own Word. Even God, Jehovah God, had to say it and believe it.

He had to exercise Faith. Did you know that God exercises his Faith? Yes! He did. He said **Let there be,** and there was. And that was God speaking the Word of Faith. God had to make a confession of Faith himself.

NOTES:

Principle #19

Faith Power is Resurrected Power.

For you to see Faith Power in action, you will have to make a confession of God's Word. You must make a confession of the Word of Faith to see the power of Faith in action and manifestation. Faith Power only comes by confession of the Word of God. Faith Power is resurrected from your spirit man because only your recreated spirit, which is a king, can exercise Faith Power. Only your spirit man can do that miracle mystery. Your born-again spirit is a king and is from a royal family. That is the family of God. God designed you that way. Your spirit man, which is God in you, as you are all God. You were created by God as a king and a Priest to function from out of those two natures. The only way you can communicate with God is from and through your born-again and recreated nature. So, you believe in God by your spirit. A lot of people are trying to believe in God from their souls. But you cannot believe in God from your soul. This is because your soul cannot understand the spirit of God. The soul does not understand what Faith is. You can only understand and see the power of God, which is Faith power, become alive through your spirit.

NOTES:

Now, how do you see? You see from the supernatural realm, not from your mind or soul, but from your spirit. When God gives you a revelation of something, He gives you that revelation through your spirit, because your soul cannot receive the things of the spirit, because your soul is made up of the will. Your soul is made up of your mind. Your soul operates out of and from your emotions and feelings. So, your soul cannot receive the things of God, because the things of God are revealed by the Spirit of God. To see the manifestation of God in action, you will have to see it from God's point of view. You must see God's point of reference as the only way to see the power of God in action. Faith is a spiritual element. That is why Faith is different from your belief. Nowhere does it say to have belief in God. It says to have Faith in God. It says without Faith it is impossible to please God. It tells us to live our lives by Faith. It says, "the Just shall live by Faith." It never said anything about belief. A lot of saints believe and think that Faith and belief have the same meaning. But this is not true. Faith is action. It is not action only, but it is one of the elements of prayer. You cannot pray without Faith. And, you must have belief in what you are praying for. Without belief, there is no thread to attach to your Faith to pull your request that you prayed for out of the supernatural into the material world. You cannot pray without Faith, just like you cannot have ice without the cold.

NOTES:

CHAPTER 7
FAITH IS ALWAYS A CONTRADICTION

Principle #21

Faith is Always a Contradiction.

Luke 5:4-7says

4. Now, when he had left speaking, he said unto Simon, Launch out into the deep, and let down your nets for a draught.

5. And Simon answering said unto him, Master, we have toiled all the night, and have taken nothing: nevertheless, at thy word I will let down the net.

6. And when they had this done, they inclosed a great multitude of fishes: and their net brake.

7. And they beckoned unto their partners, which were in the other ship, that they should come and help them. And they came, and filled both the ships, so that they began to sink.

Toiling all night and catching nothing was a very upsetting situation for these fishermen. Now! There were two fishing boats in this fishing area. None of these fishermen had a good fishing experience on this fishing journey. Usually, experienced fishermen know where to go for a great catch. But, on this night, they toiled and toiled all night out in the deep seas without a catch. I believe it was about six o'clock in the morning when they all had sad faces because they weren't successful with their fishing. And Jesus shows up on the scene and tells them to cast their nets out into the deep. Now, let us look at the circumstances here. They knew Jesus as the carpenter, and they were fishermen. Here comes this carpenter telling them, well-experienced fishermen, where to throw their nets, especially after a long night of catching nothing. Ready to go home, this doesn't seem right, and sure enough, it doesn't sound right.

NOTES:

If that were some of us, we would have said, later for that. We would have said, "You are a carpenter." What do you know about fishing? They could have made excuses for their disappointment, but they all made a choice to be obedient to the voice of the Lord. "Master, we have toiled all the night and have taken nothing; nevertheless, at thy word I will let down the net". Nevertheless, that was the keyword. He said at thy Word, lord. I will let down the nets. Simon didn't let the circumstance dictate his outcome. Even though he had the experience of all-night toiling without any catch, he was sure enough to do what the fisher of men told him to do. Who was this man? What did he know that we didn't know? What had he seen beneath the water? Had he seen a school of fish swimming by? Simon didn't let that bother him. He said, At thy Word, Lord. When he had done this, they had enclosed a great multitude of fish. They had so many fish that their net broke. Imagine if Peter had said, "No, Lord, we have been here all night long and haven't caught anything. We will come back later; maybe tonight we will have a better chance of a catch. We are going home to sleep."

He didn't let his circumstances dictate his outcome. God wants us to do the same thing today. He wants us to stay at thy Word, Lord. One of the reasons why we are not receiving the blessing of the lord is because we are not affirming the statement "at thy word, Lord".

NOTES:

Principle #23

God Means What He says.

When God says at thy Word, Lord, He means what He says. If He said for you to walk left, He means to walk left. That is Faith in action. Jesus sees your Faith in your actions. So, in other words, your actions represent your Faith. Act on what God tells you to do. It may not be what you understand it to be. But act, act, and act on what God's Word says, and you will receive the reward for your action. Don't try to figure out God. Faith sees the answers when fear and doubt avails. Faith sees through the spirit. When the mind and the soul are trying to figure it out, Faith sees. When everyone around you is trying to see their way, Faith sees your answers. When everyone around you is trying to figure things out, you will say I know it, I receive it, I believe it, I confess it, and I accept it.

Why can you stand on your affirmation? It is because you see it already completed in the spiritual realm as God sees it. So, develop your spiritual eyes of Faith.

NOTES:

Mark 11:22-24 says

22. Jesus, answering saith unto them, Have Faith in God.

If Jesus said for you to have Faith in God, that means you can have Faith in God. It means that you do not have to struggle to have Faith in God. That means you can have the God kind of Faith to believe God for anything you desire to have according to God's will and purpose for your life.

23. For verily I say unto you, That whosoever shall say unto this mountain, Be thou removed, and be thou cast into the sea; and shall not doubt in his heart, but shall believe that those things which he said shall come to pass, he shall have whatsoever he saith.

Whosoever meant you and me. It doesn't say white man, black man, male man, female man, the man, or the other man. It said *and shall not doubt in his heart*. The heart referred to in this passage is your mind. If you believe in your spirit, those things which he saith shall come to pass; he shall have whatsoever he saith. Whatsoever is like whosoever. Whatsoever means everything, and whosoever means everyone. So, whatever you say, that is what you are going to have.

NOTES:

Principle #25

Act Like you Received the Things you Desire.

24. Therefore I say unto you, What things soever you desire, when ye pray, believe that you receive them, and ye shall have them.

Act like you have received the things you asked of God. That is what God wants us to do. Act like you already received it. See it happening for you just as God said it would happen. Visualize it as you would like it to be. Then begin to say it out of your mouth. Get a visual picture of that thing you are asking God for. If it is home, get a picture of a home that represents the home you want to have. Place it somewhere in your bedroom where you can see it every day. Then make it a daily ritual, at the same time each day, if possible, to confess and affirm that you are at home. See yourself in the home walking around and decorating it as you like. Thank God that He keeps his promise while you work at speaking Faith in action. Now! Faith involves work and action. You work in your actions. Action is believing in God's Word. Can you work without action? I don't think you can. In the natural realm, you must work with action. It is the same way in the spiritual realm. When the spirit of doubt comes, speak to that spirit of doubt and tell it to go in Jesus' Name. Dethrone the spirit of doubt.

NOTES:

Principle #26

An Established Man is a Full Man.

A man established by God is a man of full stature. Let God establish you in all things. When you are established by God, you will be able to follow His directions he has for you. Obedience will follow establishment in the things of God. When you are obedient to God's work and his voice, you will be able to step into your destiny. You will begin to experience the receiving power of the Almighty God, standing firm on what you are seeing in the spirit.

Proverb 18:21; 6:2

21. Death and life are in the power of the tongue, and they that love it shall eat of the fruit thereof.

Death and life have fruits. And the Bible says that they that love it shall eat of it. The fruit of death is defeat. If you speak things into your life that do not enhance your spiritual life, they will automatically produce defeat and eventually death. You have the creative ability of God. God has placed the power of death and life in the ability of your tongue. So, begin to create and declare your destiny and walk in the kingdom authority that belongs to you.

NOTES:

Principle #27
Don't be Trapped by Your Words.

6:2 Thou art snared with the words of thy mouth, and thou art taken with the words of thy mouth

The word snared means to be taken as a trap. It is being trapped by your own words. Your words are your bond. You are bound by your words. Better stated, a snare is a trap set for capturing animals. Sometimes you will put yourself in positions that will bind you up by the things that you say. Your words are powerful tools you can choose to use for God or the enemy. Your words are spirit and can only operate on the level it was designed to function within. Spirit works with the Word and words of man. If you say the wrong things, you will get the wrong results. Watch your confession. If you believe the wrong thing, you will get the wrong results. But, if you're thinking is right, you would believe right, and you would have that which is righteous, good, and blessed. Renew your mind with the Word of God and let those things God has in store for you come to pass in this realm. So, words are powerful. Words operate on the same plane as spirits. What you say is what you get, and what you get you will never forget. Make the right confession of Faith. Follow the right belief because believing will always bring you to the level of receiving. So, if you have the wrong things in your life, then it must be that you believed God for the wrong things. If you believed God for the wrong things, then you can only get what you have believed for. Your mind must be renewed by the Word of God. The Word of God is spiritual food for thought.

NOTES:

CHAPTER 8
MANIFESTED FAITH IS LIVING BY FAITH

Principle #28

Let the Word of Christ Dwell in You.

What does the Word of God say before asking? Well! It says to abide in me, and if my words abide in you. You can ask anything in my name. There is something that must be done prior to your asking for anything.

John 15:7 says

7. If ye abide in me, and my words abide in you, ye shall ask what ye will, and it shall be done unto you.

What does it say before asking? It says if ye abide in me, and if my words abide in you. So, we see from this passage of scripture that there is something which must be done before we can ask. And that something is abiding in Christ and letting Christ abide in us. And then we can ask for what we will, and it shall be done unto you. Do you see the requirements? We have something to do. In other words, we must be connected to the vine. The branch and the vine must be connected to each other.

If we do not abide in him, we cannot ask of him. What kind of relationship would it be if you abide in him and he is not abiding in you? You see, just as God and His Word are one, we and Jesus are one. Well! We must abide in Jesus, and Jesus must abide in us. And the Bible says, Whatsoever ye ask? What will happen? It shall be done.

NOTES:

Principle #29

Christ is all Truth.

This is a strong statement I am indicating here. I want you to understand this well. I want you to receive this in your spirit. If Christ abides in us, then we are going to be clothed with his truth. The Word of God tells us that Christ is the truth. And if we abide in him, and His Word abides in us, then we are going to be clothed with truth. The Bible says that the truth shall set us free. So then, if the truth will set us free and we are in Him, and His Word is in us, then Faith can absolutely have a perfect work in our lives. Remember, Jesus Christ is the way, the truth, and the life. Jesus Christ fulfills all truth. What I like about this truth is Jesus Christ fulfills every promise that he has promised that he made. He is embodied with truth. And the truth of the matter is that his promises are truth. So, if we abide in him and His Word abides in us, we can obtain all his promises by the Word of Faith. If we are abiding in him, and he abides in us, what is happening is that there is a level of obedience. But if we don't abide in him, and he doesn't abide in us, we will be asking amiss. If we ask amiss, we cannot receive because we will not be operating in the God kind of Faith. In other words, we must take the place of Jesus on this earth and manifest the power of God. What I am saying to you is simple. You and I must take Jesus' place in his absence on this earth.

NOTES:

Principle #30

We Are the Jesus' That the World Sees.

We are the only Jesus that the world is going to see. Jesus abides in you so that you can bear his light and see the light of the Father through the image of the Son. Jesus is the revelation of God, and we are the revelation of Jesus on the earth. For the man to see Jesus, they must see Him in us. How do they see Jesus in us? They must see the light manifest through us. Start acting like Jesus acted, speaking like Jesus spoke, and doing as Jesus did. The Bible says that Jesus is the light of all men. Jesus lived a life of obedience. At no time written in the Gospels does it indicate that Jesus was not obedient. Even up to the last hour, Jesus was obedient. To be obedient, you must be willing. There are times when you can be obedient but not willing. Or you can be willing and not obedient. But Jesus fulfilled these two requirements. All throughout his ministry, he fulfilled these requirements. It was because of this that Jesus didn't pray for the sick as we do today. He didn't have to pray long, drawn-out prayers for the sick and the afflicted. He didn't have any drawn-out deliverance services. Why? He had the God kind of Faith and lived a life of obedience. And the result of his willingness and obedience, all He had to do was speak. He spoke to the waters, and the waters obeyed him. He spoke to nature, and the wind stopped.

NOTES:

Faith Principles
For Manifesting Your Prophetic Word
Terrence Parris, PhD and Willie Mae Parris, PhD

In conclusion, Jesus, we know, was the expressed image of the Father. Though Jesus was born of a woman, in the form of human flesh, He was also the express image of God. The Apostle Paul took special note of this powerful fact in his epistle to the Hebrews. Jesus was the brightness of God's Glory. Just as Jesus fixed His Faith on the infallible and impregnable Word of God, you and I must do the same today. There are many Christians who are too busy to get in the Word and stay in the Word. They have their eyes on preachers and teachers and are accepting everything that echoes out of their mouths.

Everyone must be able to stand on their ground and know what the Word of God says concerning their Faith in the Lord Jesus Christ. They must carry the same shield of Faith that Jesus used to defeat Satan. **Hebrews 12:2 says, looking unto Jesus the author and finisher of our faith; who for the joy that was set before him endured the cross, despising the shame, and is set down at the right hand of the throne of God.**

When problems and cares of this life seem to overwhelm you, you may think, "If only my Faith were stronger, I would be able to win this battle". Just as Jesus won his battles, you and I can win our battles. Jesus, by Faith in the Word, defeated Satan in the wilderness. By Faith, He performed miracles. He healed the sick, the blind, and the deaf. He raised the dead. By Faith, He proclaimed the Word of life over death and won the battle with principalities and powers. In Him, you have the same conquering Faith that enabled Him to conquer the enemy. Not only is Jesus the author and perfecter of Faith. God's plans for you are for you to grow up into Him. In all things, He wants you to face every battle carrying the same mighty shield of Faith Jesus used to defeat the Devil. How do you develop Faith? Faith cometh by hearing the Word of God. How do we activate our Faith? It is activated when we act on what the Word says. Through nature, we understand that the world and everything alive in it were created by the hands of God. And that means that you do not have to struggle to have Faith in God. Faith is the substance of all things hoped for, the evidence of those things not seen. Thank God for FAITH; without Faith, none of us will be able to please God.

QUESTIONS FOR REVIEW

Chapter 1. Faith Cometh by Hearing

1. What does the Bible say Faith is?

2. How does the Bible say for us to walk?

3. How does Faith come?

4. Do you know why Faith is always present?

5. How can your Faith be measured?

6. Without Faith, it is impossible to please God. Please explain.

7. What arena does Faith operate in?

8. What builds Faith?

9. Is trust related to Faith? Please explain.

10. Why is it important to hear the Word of God?

11. Explain in your own words the difference between negative and positive Faith.

12. Why do so many Christians get involved in occult practices?

13. What are your perceptions about doubt and belief?

14. Does God ever sleep?

15. Define the following words: Faith, Foolishness, and Presumption.

16. Give an example of the two sides of Faith.

17. Give an example of a time you underestimated God in your life.

18. You are the person that you are because of what Christ did for you. What did Christ do for you by His death at Calvary?

19. Distractions from the outside world are designed to do what to the Child of God?

20. Your ear is a doorway to the spirit world. Please explain.

21. Explain John 1:1.

22. What is revelation and how does a person receive it?

23. Who reveals the Word to you?

24. What have you learned about yourself thus far?